A Pocket Full of Crumbs

Iona 20. 8. 16

For Polly + Ron
with thanks for the
inspiration of the
Fallen Christ —
and many insights +
conversations

love - Jan

For my family and friends, who challenge, inspire and encourage

– and actually read my poetry

A Pocket Full of Crumbs

Jan Sutch Pickard

wild goose
publications

www.**ionabooks**.com

First published 2016 by
Wild Goose Publications,
21 Carlton Court
Glasgow, G5 9JP, UK
the publishing division of the Iona Community.
Scottish Charity No. SC003794.
Limited Company Reg. No. SC096243.

ISBN 978-1-84952-484-1

Cover image and internal photos © Anja Jardine

Overseas distribution
Australia: Willow Connection Pty Ltd, Unit 4A, 3-9 Kenneth Road,
Manly Vale, NSW 2093
New Zealand: Pleroma, Higginson Street, Otane 4170, Central Hawkes Bay
Canada: Novalis/Bayard Publishing & Distribution, 10 Lower Spadina Ave.,
Suite 400, Toronto, Ontario M5V 2Z2

Printed by Bell & Bain, Thornliebank, Glasgow

Contents

Introduction   9

Broken bread   13

Curve of a human hand   16
A glimpse of Gaza   17
Flabella   18
Today   19
Just breathing   19
Like an olive tree (for Isabel)   20
A pocket full of crumbs   21

Down to earth   23

Blackhouses, lighthouses   25
Rainbow at Craignure   26
Brambles from the broch   27
'Ripeness is all'   27
Good cloth, well-cut   28
The potato poem   29
Drouth   31
Feet on the ground   32
Thumbprint   33
Work in progress   34
Primroses on the Uisken road   35

Fell to earth here   37

Heavy weather   39
Fell to earth here   39
Child's play   42

Living among legends   *43*

Colonsay graveyard   46
The journey of John Mcpherson   46
A farewell to Fiunary   47
Mediaeval frieze frame   48
St Swithun was here   49
An apple from Milton's garden   50
GH 1632   51
Scoor cave   52
The Mariota Stone   53
Ross of Mull Nativity   54
Fire-drake   55

Poems for people   *57*

Skye interior (for Ruth)   59
A day of gold and spices (for Euphie)   60
Daisies/Gowans (*Genus Compositae*) (for Margaret)   60
Butterfly orchids (for Maimie)   62
Burns on the cliffs of Burg (for Cathie)   63
Wearing purple (for Zam)   64
Throwing an egg over the house (a family story)   64
In Brighton (for Linus)   66
Surfing (for Anna)   67
The voyager (for Dwin)   68
The little waves (for Erin)   70

'The Parlement of foules'   *71*

Seagulls on the strand   73
The ringed plover   73
Whooper swans   74

Listening to Lunga   74
Iona rookery   76
The flyting   77
The white blackbird   78
Swallows at Crianlarich   80
The Staffa corncrake   81
The Penmon robin   82
Midwinter wren   83
Listening for larks   84

Writing desk on the shore   85

The writing desk   87
Beach pebble   88
Lighthouse design   89
Collaroy beach   90
Uisken   91
Flotsam   92
A can of worms   93
WARNING – 'Don't turn your back on the waves'   94
Walk by its side   95

Introduction

I sat down to write this introduction in such haste that I haven't taken off my coat. I put my hand into my pocket just now – and found it full of crumbs. Where do they come from? Yesterday I went over to Iona to the Communion Service in the Abbey Church. Afterwards I needed to walk briskly down the road to lead worship in the Parish Church before doing the same back home on the Ross of Mull. But first I was grateful to receive the ministry of word and music, bread and wine. And oatcakes.

It's a terrible habit, putting food into my pocket. Yesterday it happened like this: at the end of the service, as the congregation left the Abbey Church, some of the folk who had served Communion were at the doors, offering baskets of oatcakes, for each of us to take one to share with a stranger. This, which may be an ancient Celtic tradition, is certainly a good way of getting into conversation with someone you meet in the cloisters in Iona, like Miriam, cook at the MacLeod Centre, as she offered a basket full of freshly baked, fragrant oatcakes. I shared mine with a guest from the Netherlands. But it's hard to eat and have a conversation – especially when there are so many questions to ask and words to find, especially when time is ticking away. So half a nibbled oatcake was slipped into my pocket.

This keeps happening: where the midpoint of an Iona Community pilgrimage is marked, on the machair, by welcome flapjack, at beach picnics with my family sharing sandy sandwiches. When I was an Ecumenical Observer – a peace monitor – on the West Bank, I was given flatbread from the *taboon* – the earth-oven – of my Muslim neighbours; in West Jerusalem, the Women in Black shared cookies at the end of a stressful demonstration; after church in Nablus, Palestinian Christians lingered over coffee: but I'm not good at eating and talking. The morsels go into my pocket – and later become food for the birds.

This collection of poems can be compared to such crumbs – from many sources. They are reminders of encounters and conversations, of walks along lonely beaches and long waits at checkpoints in the Separation Barrier on the West Bank when I was an Ecumenical Accompanier there. They have the taste of the life that I share with the birds of the air and human beings with their feet on muddy ground. Some connect with poems published earlier, in *Out of Iona* or *Between High and Low Water* (Wild Goose), being set in the same places, becoming more familiar year by year, but never taken for granted – for these are still songs of a sojourner. In *Between High and Low Water* I wrote this:

> *I am a sojourner – that's a beautiful and ancient word, but what does it mean today? I live on the island of Mull, in a community where many of my neighbours have deep roots, whereas I grew up in a family constantly on the move. Here I'll always be an incomer. Folk are accepting; I hope to become a contributing member of the community; at the same time I know I belong to a wider world. Travelling away from time to time, I come back with stories of other landscapes, communities and cultures, to set alongside those that belong on the Ross of Mull. Outsiders are expected to ask awkward questions, so I do, sometimes. In return, my neighbours, while making me welcome, ask, 'Will you stay? Can you ever settle down or are you just passing through?' In the church as much as in the village street, I know I'm an incomer, a bird of passage, a resident alien, one who makes a temporary stay among others: a sojourner.*

In common with many folk at the beginning of the twenty-first century, I'm living across cultures and sometimes, as a Christian, counter-culturally. We find ourselves in a time of transition, between the tides of history. So the expanse of the foreshore – where I walk most days – is a powerful symbol for me: it is open to constant change, the stones and wrack swept in and out, sandbanks reconfigured, moving waters, restless flights of birds …

Some of these poems have appeared in print in a series of small pamphlets called Gatherings, produced with the idea that people find poetry in small quantities less intimidating! A gathering is a piece of parchment or vellum, folded and cut to make sixteen pages or eight spreads – the basic unit of a mediaeval manuscript. This nugget of information might not seem very applicable to daily life in the twenty-first century, even in the Hebrides, almost certainly the birthplace of the Book of Kells. On Iona the 'little book' of the Bible was read and written out, word by word, under the curving roof of a beehive cell – while all around, on this and neighbouring islands, the 'great book' of creation turned its pages by day and night and through the seasons. And still does. So when I write I'm celebrating these places where, even alone, I feel so much alive. I'm celebrating, then and now, the presence of other human beings: those who laboured to make books – their craft skills, creativity and stubborn faith – and those in whose lives I read God at work and am nourished. I'm celebrating the power of words and imagination, even in our chaotic and broken world, and my own faith in a God who is the living and life-giving Word.

But how can I hold these together – all this sustenance from so many different sources, all these words? In the very first Gathering I wrote this:

Chester Beaty MS

Like an urgent message
on the back of an envelope
this papyrus fragment
records Jesus' words from the cross:
'Woman, behold your son.'
It was written only 50 years
after the death of John,
that beloved friend, adopted son, solitary scribe
who gives his name to the Gospel
from which this handful of words
has come crumpled
out of the back pocket of time.

And now I want to add to this my own urgent message about 'a pocket full of crumbs' (p.21):

Now I hold these crumbs in cupped hands,
remembering those who baked the bread

and blessed it by sharing:
this way nothing is wasted, this way
I find words in what is broken and lost.

Jan Sutch Pickard,
Bunessan, Mull,
April 2016

Broken bread

Here's a handful of poems which give glimpses of injustice, conflict and human goodness in Israel/Palestine. I sit down to write an introduction. What more can I say? I try to focus on what I've learned, in a few visits, which has moved me so much. But I'm distracted by an e-mail asking me to write a few words for a prayer handbook.

I offer this prayer:

With-us God, you came to share our human lives
in Bethlehem – 'the house of bread'.
We pray for those who bake bread and break it
on both sides of the wall of separation:
Jewish families gathered for the Shabbat meal,
Christian and Muslim Palestinians
sharing flatbread fresh from the taboun.
You are Living Bread, broken that all might be fully alive,
so we pray for the day when all your children
will be free to share their daily bread together, in peace.
Amen

These poems connect places of pilgrimage – the islands of the Inner Hebrides and the land that we call Holy. An earlier Gathering, *Holy Places*, was inspired by *De Locis Sanctis*, written by Adomnán, a successor to Columba as abbot of the Celtic community in Iona, about the Holy Land which he had never seen, as described by a returning pilgrim (blown off course) who found refuge on Iona. In this century, I've sat under the curving roof of a ruined beehive hut on an uninhabited island near Iona, thinking of the hermit to whom it was space and sanctuary. On Mull, I can see the same curve in the roof of a recycled Anderson shelter. It's like a human hand – raised in protection: an image from today's wars in the Middle East.

Another shape intrigued me – the flabella, fans with little bells for liturgical use. They appear in the Book of Kells, in the hands of angels. I thought they belonged in that remote past. Then, attending an Eastern Rite service in East Jerusalem, I realised where that chime of tiny bells was coming from: a small solace for folk whose life outside the church walls was challenging in so many ways.

Serving as an Ecumenical Accompanier, I wrote about travelling across the West Bank by bus, helping to monitor the daily queues of workers at the Gilo Checkpoint on the edge of Bethlehem, working alongside farmers to plant sapling olive trees. In the olive groves I heard of the death of a friend, Isabel, far away, and found a connection. Close at hand, meanwhile, strangers – Palestinian and Israeli – were my companions, sharing food, breaking bread: in worship, on demonstrations, in daily life.

Curve of a human hand

Curve of a human hand
warding off danger:
symbol of shelter, more than a gesture –
stretched as far as a curve can,
fragile, resilient, and
a shape we know in our bones;

sixty years ago, jetsam of war
was put to good use from Tiraghoil to Kintra:
there's still an Anderson shelter on most crofts –
nothing is wasted here –
so these little sheds house chickens,
store onions, keep tools from rust;
thrawn, rusting themselves,
humble structures with bowed roofs, just
like the curve of a human hand …

thirteen centuries have passed
but on the Garvellachs
the beehive huts still stand, battered
by time and sea winds, but not demolished;
like chambered shells, broken open
showing the beauty of their convolutions;
places to read creation's great book,
space to turn the eye inward,
refuge from the wind's fury
and angry clamour of the news;
skilfully built, the subtle arch of the roof – look –
like the curve of a human hand …

minutes ago, more shellfire;
a bomb explodes over huddled houses
far from these peaceful islands;
in a war that threatens us all,
we glimpse people with no refuge –
in Gaza, right now,
the camera gazes into the terrified eyes
of a woman holding her child, while
the other hand's raised ...

the curve of a human hand
warding off the raging world,
stretched as far as a curve can:
a little refuge of humanity,
resilient, fragile, and
more than a gesture, a symbol of shelter –
this shape we know in our bones.

A glimpse of Gaza

Beyond intensively green fields – a land cultivated
for all its worth (we have ways of making
the desert bloom) – and past
barbed wire and thorny scrub, beyond
low sandy hills, pale buildings out of focus,
complicated
cluster of communication masts:
ragged edges of a city in the heat haze,

like a dream on the edge of waking –
dislocated –
a different reality
getting lost in the hard light of day.
Beyond belief.
Dust, poppies, distant gunfire ...
beyond, the sea.

Yes, this is Gaza, no mistaking:
tears blur words fail. Gaze

Flabella

(East Jerusalem, January 2010)

Shaken not by an angel
in the Book of Kells, long ago,
but by a grey-haired acolyte
in a congregation in Jerusalem, here and now:
a chime like ice falling
from the twigs of birch trees as the sun rises;
incense rising like mist
as the priest breaks the Host.
January sun streams through high windows
and 'Light of light' sing the people
in their Sunday best, in Arabic, and after
the acolyte by the candled altar
shakes the flabellum once more
above bright Sunday faces,
so the little bells resound
like angels' laughter.

Today

Today I saw a soldier in a prayer shawl,
with gun and phylactery and book,
bowing behind the Humvee, beside the barbed wire
of the Separation Barrier: for him, maybe
as good – or bad – as any other place to pray,
today.

Today I travelled on a bus
where every passenger (coming tired from work)
greeted the driver and each other with
'Peace be upon you – and upon you, peace';
while the driver, who played *dabke* music all the way,
noticed the dove and cross on my vest
and wouldn't let me pay –
today.

Just breathing

Dark and cold before dawn, where men,
who rose much earlier, are waiting to go to work,
packed into long narrow pens that run
the length of the ramp, along that concrete wall,
scrawled with scorn and defiance: though in the dark
no-one can see the writing on the wall;
nor can you see the faces of these men
huddled together, leaning on the wire fence
which bulges with the weight of humanity
barely contained; all you can see is – here

a hand grasping a bar – there
breath puffed out in the chill air;
or spidering forms against the sky, trying to climb
into a cage already crammed, through razor wire;
weary with standing still for more than an hour,
a score of men are sitting down on the ground
by common consent, shoulder to shoulder,
their upturned faces catching what light there is;
here someone coughs … over there
a man lights a cigarette and passes it round;
no-one is talking – what is there to say?
Yet, filling the dark, a shapeless sound like grieving:
seven hundred men waiting for someone to open a gate,
hoping for a way out, and just breathing.

Like an olive tree

(for Isabel)

Like an olive tree
that has stood the test of time,
whose leaves flicker like pale flames,
seeming faded in strong sunlight: silvered, dry,
but still growing, full of life and the sun's energy.

Like an olive tree
that, when it is cut down,
springs up green from the root,
begins again, patiently, goes on bearing fruit.

Like an olive tree
that marks boundaries, connects
communities, embodies neighbourliness,
and is cherished by generations – a family tree –
tradition-bearing, sharing stories rich with meaning,
sheltering, welcoming with solace and good food.

Like an olive tree
now you're transplanted to a place
where none of us has yet set foot, a garden
where trees have healing leaves, saints meet and rejoice …

Oh, but we miss you here, your voice, your face,
your generous grace, your steadfastness for peace.

A pocket full of crumbs

In the middle of a conversation,
I put my hand in my pocket
and find it full of crumbs.

They belong together – words and bread –
but I don't always find it easy
to cope with both at once:

to give full, serious attention
to food offered in love, while finding
and savouring the right words.

So, from time to time,
I slip a morsel into my pocket
instead of into my mouth.

Now what's here? A crust
torn from the flatbread, that our neighbour
broke by the brazier on a cold morning,
and a piece of the bread
shared by Christians in Nablus
at close of Sunday worship,
and a cookie from the Women in Black
after their Friday demonstration:
such different meanings – mingled

in crumbs now. What can I do?
Bread is holy, I can't throw it away.
But, while it is always better

to eat today's bread companionably,
now I hold these crumbs in cupped hands,
remembering those who baked the bread

and blessed it by sharing:
this way nothing is wasted, this way
I find words in what is broken and lost.

Down to earth

These pieces are planted in the soil of Mull and Iona: mud that grows brambles and primroses, clay that makes pots and people, rock that built homes and lighthouses. They don't really need explanations. But I'd like to celebrate where the quirky 'potato poem' came from. The National Trust ran a project, Changing Landscapes, bringing students from Oban High School to Iona – a place that many of them had never visited. Staying at the Iona Hostel for a couple of nights, sixth-formers from the School of Traditional Music, and others who were studying creative writing, explored the island, listened to its stories, experimented with musical and written responses, put together a performance in the Abbey.

As one of the tutors, I accompanied them, telling some local history tales. As they sat and wrote, so did I, moved by the here-and-now of mutual learning that happened when we visited Iona Primary School. Pupils there had asked their grandparents and older neighbours on the island about their memories of harvest. It was a lively morning as the little ones proudly showed the older students round the school garden and their raised beds, naming many things that grow in the fertile, storied earth of Iona.

Blackhouses, lighthouses

People who lived in blackhouses
could just about tell pot from kettle
by touch in the sooty dusk;
all was familiar, snug as a much-slept-in bed,
the air thick with peat, fish-oil, kale, kippers,
damp tweed and the byre's musk.

Folk from the blackhouses
must have been astonished by lighthouses:
suddenly vertical on the sea horizon,
built out there with such skill, so many risks;
or closer at hand, at the cliff's edge,
a tower heretically high, reaching for the clouds,
at night its beam cutting the dark like a knife.

They were dazzled by lime-wash, symmetry
of keepers' cottages ranged on either side
of the hyperbolic tower; strange white
houses with glass windows and high chimneys,
so the reek streamed away on the wind:
leaving each home austere, swept bare,
breathing out the old, breathing in the light.

Rainbow at Craignure

Waiting for the ferry on a grey day that's longing for spring,
when – looming through mid-Sound mist and myopic smirr –
MV Isle of Mull comes into the jetty, finding her berth.

Ropes thrown are caught and go taut; when the ramp goes down,
cars and vans emerge from the belly of the whale,
while the not-quite-state-of-the-art gangway creeps and bleeps
into place for the tramp of feet, of people with pushchairs,
shopping trolleys, cases on wheels, tool-bags, backpacks;
with dogs, with walking poles, on crutches, eagerly, wearily;
in anoraks and overalls, funeral black and island castaways,
all human life is here, disembarking or going aboard;
those arriving waving to those going away, cheerily:
the island emptying and filling as its people come and go,
flow and counter-flow, like tides, seasons, nights, days,
with endings that are also beginnings.

And now, out of the mist, the gift of a rainbow,
on this grey day, ordinary day, the birthday of spring.

Brambles from the broch

Sweet, with a savour of the salt wind,
fruit of a second blessing of sunshine;
as autumn sets in, brambles cluster,
succulent, lustrous, in the shelter of this broch:
tumbled stones still making a *caim* –
a circle of protection –
where right now a rowan offers berries for the birds,
a wild rose flaunts its hips
and these brambles,
making themselves at home between these walls,
have prepared, against the winter,
a preserve in the pot of the broch.

'Ripeness is all'

All the way to the wedding
along the rough track
I was picking brambles and tasting them.
Some were tender and full of juice,
some still hard
and tart on the tongue.
In marriage, too, sweetness
can't be taken for granted.
But sometimes it takes you by surprise
with maturity
and generous goodness.

Good cloth, well-cut

Wind from the North –
we turn our backs to it,
waiting for the ferry
which will soon return all these folk
to the real world.

There was a funeral
on Mull today –
though all there's to show for it now,
is solid citizens in black.
Hard-working men and women
in unfamiliar formal coats:
doing the decent thing
in good cloth, well-cut.
Men and women with tight faces
which today have wept
in the cold wind,
or smiled too much
at near-strangers.

The wind from the North
persists, seeking out the cracks,
nagging like a hollow tooth,
trying to get too close,
making us wonder about going
any further from warm hearths
when the island is home.

But having paid their last respects,
seeing someone to their long home,
the folk in black have seen the worst
the wind can do.
It has taken their breath away.

The potato poem

Colleen, Milva, Maris Peer –
potatoes have names, too,
like places on this island,
like people who work the land –
names and meanings.
>   *One potato, two potato, three potato, four*
>   *Five potato, six potato, seven potato, more …*

In the schoolyard,
Cameron and his friend
grew potatoes in their raised bed
among carrots, candytuft and beans:
'But now we've harvested them.'
>   *One potato, two potato, three potato, four*
>   *Five potato, six potato, seven potato, more …*

Each October, years ago,
island families took time off school
to lift the potatoes on the croft.
'Everyone worked together,' said Davie,
'including the children.'

> *One potato, two potato, three potato, four*
> *Five potato, six potato, seven potato, more …*

Further back still, a grim story:
'The year the potato went away' –
blight blackened the haulms,
the whole crop rotted in the ground;
hungry folk left their homes.
> *One potato, two potato, three potato, four*
> *Five potato, six potato, seven potato, more …*

Down-to-earth life, with moments
of wonder: Dugald MacArthur,
carting kelp from the shore
for his lazy beds, stumbled
on the pillow-stone of a saint.
> *One potato, two potato, three potato, four*
> *Five potato, six potato, seven potato, more …*

And today, we've walked back
to the hostel, hungry –
with heads full of stories –
to find a long table set
and baked potatoes galore …
> *One potato, two potato, three potato, four*
> *Five potato, six potato, seven potato, more …*

Drouth

Sky's a bonny blue
but faded by days of sun;
weather's still fine,
wind's as dry as a bone,
clouds billow like linen on a line …
and out in the public space
of this cloister/drying green
we're hanging out our washing –
threadbare but clean.

Today, away across glitter-ball waves,
dolphins were holding a ceilidh,
while in clifftop burrows
puffins got on with their chores,
chuntering away to their fellows;
now, content with a day well spent,
feel the breath-taken sky exhale,
blowing the Staffa boat back home
full of folk to tell the tale.

Tomorrow the skies may darken
and lightning flash – too soon
the wind may be full of tears –
but on this given day,
we're delighting in drouth;
so in the open space
of this cloister/drying green
we're hanging out our washing –
threadbare but clean.

Feet on the ground

It was red mud, red as Adam,
and it sucked the shoes right off my feet,
so I stood barefoot –
or at least in holey socks –
on the cold and mucky ground.

It was New Year's Day
and I was trying to make my way back
to polite people in a chill church,
with a story about the heaven's glory
and wise men following a star.

Now I was stopped in my tracks,
looking foolish and laughing helplessly
at this unexpected gift
of having to get my hands dirty
saving my shoes.

Sheep grazed, unimpressed,
clouds unfurled overhead,
sudden light struck the sea horizon –
and then and there I found
more than my footwear.

The stars still sang in their courses,
while in worship

the words that came to me
were down-to-earth:
since I'd stood on just-as-holy ground
with mud between my toes.

Thumbprint

From the menu I order apple pie;
it comes hot from the oven, fragrant,
and I see how the baker
sealed the goodness in
by pressing round the edge of the tawny crust –
decorating her handiwork simply,
with the print of her thumb.

On the dig this morning we unearthed,
with patience and careful trowel,
a fragment of a pot, lying cold in the ground,
tawny against the dark soil;
and we saw that the long-dead potter
had decorated the rim simply,
pressing down on the pliant clay –
leaving the print of her thumb.

Work in progress

Slate calls to granite
across the moving waters –
a few sea miles, but
a giant step in geology.

Granite calls to slate,
with schist and shale
and sheer basalt cliffs
falling in between.

Slate calls to granite
where the land has been gouged out,
where the sea licks its wounds.

Granite calls to slate
where red rock bares its breast,
where lighthouses were born.

At Camas Tuath on Mull
the quarrymen's homes,
built of the stone they hewed out,
are roofed with big slates –
sea-grey, set with gold
from Cullipool on Luing.

Granite calls to slate,
telling stories of hard graft
and human community.

Slate calls to granite,
across the moving waters
granite calls to slate.

Primroses on the Uisken road

Among the dead brambles
on the edge of a ditch
in this bleak wind – right now –
primroses are blooming.

First there was one alone,
a brave promise of new life,
a single star; then ten, a score,
more, more, lifting up their heads:
a constellation, a celebration –
here and now.

Though this wind chills to the bone,
between the thorns and the mud
the rumour of resurrection spreads –
there's no stopping it now.

Fell to earth here

Fallen Christ, a sculpture in granite, was given to Iona – the island and the community – in 2008. It was a joint gift from Jim Hughes and the sculptor Ronald Rae. It's now sited on crofting land beside the fence of the MacLeod Centre. In this carefully chosen place it is also outside the vallum – the boundary of the Celtic monastery. By the time all the documents were signed and arrangements made Jim was terminally ill and it was midwinter – not a good time for moving a huge piece of granite across the Sound of Iona. But it arrived and he was able to see it lowered into place. His ashes are scattered there, as are those of his wife, Margaret (Maggie), who walked here for a time of reflection every day she was on Iona, until her death in 2015.

Through her work and many friendships, Maggie knew about the plight – and potential – of people who live on the edge – believing that Iona can offer a safe place where God's children can be fully alive. So the last poem in this sequence, written when a group living with poverty and family stress were staying at the MacLeod Centre for a week, is a glimpse of one child at play.

Heavy weather

Heavy swell in the Sound. Will the ferry run?
We stand on the wrong side, frustrated and chilled to the bone.
Low clouds scud by, crows and gulls gale-blown.
Below us on the shore the great split rock is dumb
and going nowhere, on this wild and grieving day –
the greedy wind snatching our breath away.

But we've come carrying a credo, a carving in stone
which is on a journey, is finding its home:
a heavy burden that cannot be set down, ever,
until it makes land, where earth and heaven touch.
And now, being human, being absurd and real,
we feel the difficulty and pain of crossing over,
with such a weight of love, to keep our word.

Fell to earth here

Fell to earth here
like those erratic boulders
brought over from the Ross of Mull
by the ice sheet:
covering a few miles in centuries
of scraping, grinding, sliding,
painfully commuting
before finding a footing on Iona –
rosy granite among grey gneiss –
out of place and yet at home.

So this block of stone from Kemnay –
far to the east:
quarried, commissioned, carved,
came on a long journey, taking years:
resting here, welcomed there.
It was never a dolorous way,
except for the last day
when gale matched grief
and doubt about surviving
this last mile of wild water.
But care of CalMac, made it across
and fell to earth here.

Hit the earth hard
and ah now it hurts.
Jesus is falling
under the burden of the cross,
carrying our mortality –
the concentration of our fears –
crushed under the weight
of all those words
of hope and blame and power
we lay on God.

Jesus is falling, slantwise,
like salt rain before the gale,
like sweat, like tears;
falling in silence under a grey sky
and with barely a witness.

A stone from a long way off
is pinning him down here
on muddy earth, in a field of cows,
against the fence, outside the vallum –
the boundary of blessing –
on common ground.

The glacier of time crawls on and melts.
The stone has come to rest
where it will stay
while generations pass and pause:
deciphering the story,
seeing the skill that shaped,
the faith that carried it across the water.

The love that moved
maker and made, carver and makar,
so this stray stone found
its place in the universe:
falling to earth here.

Child's play

Sun burnishes the granite,
a blessing on the stone,
making it warm as human skin
but still as hard as bone.

Sculpture of the *Fallen Christ*
like an erratic boulder:
a child at play has clambered up
to perch upon his shoulder.

She rides upon the solid rock,
joyfully, safely there:
rough stone supports her hands and feet,
the wind plays with her hair.

I see a place of refuge
for a troubled little girl:
God's back being broad enough to bear
the weight of all the world.

Living among legends

Martin Martin, who travelled through his native Hebrides in the seventeenth century, recording all that he saw – land, plants and creatures, communities and their customs, daily life and legends – was moved by an ancient cross in Oronsay to write:

> *'It has an inscription but not legible,*
> *being almost worn out by the injury of time.'*

This section starts with inscriptions on gravestones – the first in neighbouring Colonsay, and the second in Fionnphort, on the Ross of Mull:

> *Erected by D Mcpherson, Appin, in memory of his beloved son John, mate of SS Fairholm, wrecked on Tory Island 22 August 1874, aged 35 years. His body was washed ashore here – a distance of 200 miles – 19 days after.*

In Morvern, across the Sound of Mull, Fiunary is the ancestral home of George MacLeod's family. 'Farewell to Fiunary' is a poignant traditional air, from a time of emigration. Visiting the place, drawn by the legendary energy and faith of MacLeod, we found instead the shell of a building, disintegrating through *'the injury of time'*.

Further afield, a frieze carved in stone in Salisbury Cathedral; a story set in stone in another cathedral – Winchester; Milton's cottage in Chalfont St Giles, Buckinghamshire; George Herbert's grave in St Andrew's Church Bemerton, with its minimal inscription:

GH.1632

All these give glimpses of legends and life-stories.

In graffiti on the wall of a cave in Mull there's a mysterious record of human activity in prehistoric and then Columban times, while the ruined mediaeval church at Kilvickeon, nearby, contains a grave-slab with an inscription of which only four words can be read:

HIC IACET MARIOTA FILIA …

The 'Mariota Stone' has its own story – as do each of us. So at the end of this section I give my own version of a medical emergency, in this landscape where legends come alive.

Colonsay graveyard

Sea wind and lichen have erased the name,
all that remains are fragments of a tale:
he was beloved – a brother and a son –
and died in action on the Somme.

In this kempt graveyard, rank on rank of stones
measure the march of years, while time erodes
particular and painful dates –
the burn that will at last wear rocks away.

Neighbouring standing stones say even less,
with flags and bluebells as mute witnesses:
while time destroys the evidence, being unmoved
that folk once lived here and were loved.

The journey of John Mcpherson

Who would have thought it, John, beloved son?
Where did they search for your shipmates and you,
in those long weeks after the wreck?
Fairholm's cargo of coal was lost: still in her hold,
fathoms deep off Tory Island, in waters
that quenched the fire in her engines for ever.
But, after the storm, her crew
must have drifted apart under the open sky
day after day, with the gulls crying.
And for you, John, a strange star-charted voyage
on long Atlantic swells, through the same currents

that carried Columcille in his *curragh*
from Ireland so many centuries before.
Who would have thought it possible,
that after traversing so many sea-miles
(your father in his grief doubled them)
you ended up on the same shores as that saint?
He going into exile, 'seeking a desert in the sea',
you making your way home, gradually.
But your haven is here now, where you were found,
a guest in this graveyard behind the beach –
your name and your story carved deep
in grey slate that never grew in this ground.

A farewell to Fiunary

A green tide is rising:
greedy grasses, nettles and dockens tangle
with branches that overhang: sycamore, elder, oak.
Clouds, too, hang heavy on the hills of Morvern
and swallows are flying low.
Here, years of rain have melted the roof,
with slates slipping, clean-cut stones
being prised apart by saplings.
This proud house has lost heart.

Five years ago we came as pilgrims,
climbing the lane, remembering
a story of both rootedness and new beginnings:
prophetic words, a standpoint outward-looking.
Knee-deep in the lawn, we prayed.

Now, in dank tree-shadow, weeds are shoulder-high
and horizons have closed in.
Plans unmade, the thread of the story lost,
dismayed, we run from the green tide,
before we're caught and drawn under.

A bound covenanter far out on the sands,
the old manse waits for the end.
Like angry angels, midges descend.

Mediaeval frieze frame

Eve offers Adam an apple,
Adam holds up his hand,
ambiguously: either 'heaven forbid'
or 'will I, won't I?', savouring the moment …
until it comes to the crunch;

the snake is slithering widdershins
around the tree and God's out to lunch;
but he'll be back when the whole sorry story
hits the headlines, when innocent curiosity
becomes disobedience and mortal sin;

and then, the glory departed, inevitably,
Adam will take gardening leave, and Eve maternity,
leaving behind Eden, its timeless mystery
and green leaves – its divine mind-games –
to spend more time with their (human) family.

St Swithun was here

Antiphons and anthems,
banners all down the nave,
petitions and processions,
priests pacing over graves,
the organ with all stops out
and sonorous Latin prayers,
but for all that pomp and circumstance
St Swithun isn't there.

No body in a sepulchre,
no relic on display,
no sign, no shrine:
scepticism and time
have swept all trace away.
Once folk felt his presence
in this city – come rain, come shine –
but history's stolen the evidence,
and under exultant arches
the paving stones lie bare –
St Swithun's now not there.

Only a crowd of worshippers
offering an obscure prayer;
hopeful holy people
blessing the empty air.

An apple from Milton's garden

Scrumped with subversive joy on a day off –
a windfall picked up for its subtle heart-shape,
its marriage of russet and green-gold,
in the garden of someone who, by the time he lived here,
could only see such things in his mind's eye:
a tree laden with fruit, a woman beguiled
and a man amazed, astonied, blank …
the apples of God's eye.

Pocketed without a qualm –
saved to be savoured, but now too late
I see the hole where the worm entered,
going right to the heart,
though my head tells me
it could still germinate.

Glimpse this on a morning of goodbyes
after a night of frost, when the gardens
have woken white with rime while the sun,
breasting the valley rim, blinds our eyes;
touching the trees, it's the last straw:
as we shut the door, green-gold and russet leaves
fall in a sudden shower without a breath of wind –
like the words of a poem taking us by surprise.

GH 1632

Within these walls, the silence is singing:
such a narrow place.

A stone dropped at the centre, rings.

The map of the world is changing –
it no longer has edges.

Yet, on the edge of your vision, the city's pinnacle
hangs like an icicle into the winter sky:
if you jump, will you go on falling upwards?

From that height you can see
where you have been
and maybe what you could become;
the kingdoms of the earth spread, golden as buttercups;
the stones crying out – could they become bread?

But you come down the winding stair,
walk across the meadows
among willows dancing in the spring wind,

and enter this still place,
a few paces across, smelling of mildew,
tasting of a metal chalice, cold as the grave:
where the silence is singing.

Scoor cave

It's a book dropped on the shore,
long ago, forgotten at the gully's foot,
small and easily overlooked, Scoor.

It's a book upturned – clifftop spine
bound with heather roots,
stamped with gold stars of tormentil.

It's a space contained – schist slabs,
peeling apart like pages,
tell a long story: of folk far back

leaving messages, mapping the stars
by making cup and ring marks
that pock the rock like raindrops on the sea.

It's where Celtic monks left their graffiti –
boundary markers or blessings –
crosses scribbled in the margins of history.

Fugitives, clans ferrying their dead,
or pilgrims seeking a desert in the sea,
beached their little boats,

safe from the wind's howl and waves' surge,
clambered up from the shore,
into the hush of this cave, breathed the musky air:

It's where they lived between its leaves.
A marked place in creation's great book:
a little missal they held to their hearts.

Out there today, in a rising autumn wind,
ravens and gulls scatter –
scraps of paper from the bonfire of time.

The Mariota Stone

HIC IACET MARIOTA FILIA …
Here lies Mariota, daughter … no more:
her family name's been lost –
levelled by lichen, chiselled by frost.

FILIA – daughter – what did that mean:
distaff, dowry, children to bear another's name?
Who was her father – farmer, warrior, clan chief?
Her mother – nameless in her grief?

Women and their names, so often
off the record, out of sight and mind;
here's one we can hold on to –
MARIOTA – who was she?

Comely, hard-working, kind?
Womanly, with mirror and comb
like proud Anna MacLean of Iona?
The green-grey stone won't let on.

What colour was her hair?
Did she wear it braided?
Maiden washing in May dew
a face unmarked by smallpox?

We don't know. We don't know.

All we have is her name – MARIOTA –
her name and where she's buried: HIC IACET.
Here she lies, in this quiet churchyard
between green swelling hills, beside the loch

where curlews and seagulls call,
a wren scolds from the ruined wall,
and the wind lets out a long sigh –
HIC IACET MARIOTA FILIA –

the rest is silence.

Ross of Mull Nativity

A star fell from the dark sky
over an island,
striking sparks – fool's gold –
from a slate gravestone
carved long years ago.

One day good people, my neighbours,
sure of nothing
but worn paths, familiar names and faces,
gathered in a ruined church
singing in the language of heaven.

Suddenly I remembered another place,
even further back in time,
where, among ordinary folk –
shepherds and midwives,
wise men and fools –
a star fell from the dark sky.

Fire-drake

Listen! It broke through the clouds –
the gale-driven roarie-bummlers –
and came in low over the village,
growling and clattering in flight.

Now the fire-drake has landed out there on the moss,
close to the school (oh keep the children indoors);
crouching, it still roars, ready to breathe fire,
while rain flies up again, like the torrents of Burg.

Come closer! Hunched against hurly-burly, we hurry
over sodden ground, puddles reflecting
the churning turning of its fierce impatience.

Come inside: its orange flanks loom, clumsily
we clamber into the belly of this beast; gloom
swallows us, among viscera of cables and belts.

Cover your ears: the roar's deafening now:
the fire-drake paws the ground,
sidles and swings, is air-bound.

Look out: heather, dead bracken, a track,
a loch, crofts, rocks and ruins scud below,
a kirkyard overgrown,
then the sea galloping with white horses.

Being air-lifted is being neither here nor there –
hovering between
island and mainland, technology and legend,
onslaught and rescue, life and death –

hold your breath.

Poems for people

'I didn't know your daughter was a surfer.' Not at all! She'd laugh at the idea. But, watching with love, admiration and trepidation as she lives life to the full, that's the image that comes to my mind. Gentle conversations with friends and neighbours, sharing delight at rare wildflowers – or very common ones – inspire in a different way, sometimes by a simple turn of phrase. The birth of grandchildren changes all our lives and calls for more than an off-the-shelf card. Remembered experiences continue to make a connection with unique human beings. There's a lot more to say about the boat that I bought from Dwin Capstick (which can be found in the Gathering *About a Boat*, written with Joy Mead). But this poem's for Dwin. The many friends of Zam Walker, an inspiring person, know how, while she enjoyed Jenny Joseph's 'When I am an old woman I shall wear purple', Zam lived the life she was given to the full, with faith – and style. My father really *did* throw an egg over the house – and started something. Meeting an artist in Skye, I remember that sometimes pictures say more than words.

Skye interior

(for Ruth)

Two women at a kitchen table
with mugs of tea from a brown pot;
evening sunlight through a low long window
framing green leaves and seeding grass
and glowing orange lilies;
away into the distance, still water, sky and hills:
high summer
the serene colours of high summer.

On the table a paisley-patterned cloth,
on the cloth a blue bowl
full of tomatoes, a pink begonia,
two brimming mugs, not matching,
books, family photographs …

silence and stories being shared,
insights and images;
in the same way it takes two to wind
a skein of bright wool into a ball –
passing it to and fro
across a kitchen table
where two women are sitting
over mugs of tea.

A day of gold and spices

(for Euphie)

We drove along the Ross
on a mundane journey, on a day of exuberant
spring sunshine. High out of sight
exulting larks let down ladders of song
and whole hillsides were alight
with coconut-scented gorse:
flowers like a million candle flames.
'Everything's golden,' I exclaimed.
You smiled, 'Of course – "Even Solomon in all his glory
was not arrayed like one of these."'
On a day of gold and spices,
you, who I thought I knew, became for me
the Queen of Sheba in the story:
enigmatic, gifted with insight; a wise woman,
blind but mindful, taking everything in.
And cherishing on your closed eyelids
the enduring image of sixty years
of sunshine on the whin.

Daisies/Gowans (Genus Compositae)

(for Margaret)

They're bonny, they're sunny –
bring a smile to your face;
they're blooming well growing
all over the place.

In the dear green places
of the workaday city
they defy dull agendas –
subversively pretty.

Practical, focused,
with feet on the ground:
where gowans are growing
who can feel down?

On Iona's green machair –
hillock and hollow –
a path of white flowers
for pilgrims to follow:

yes, daisies know well
what keeps shows on the road;
such cheerful companions
help lighten the load,

like down-to-earth folk,
with no pomp or pretence:
just experience embodied
and good common sense.

Genus Compositae:
this flower you see
is amazingly complex –
a community!

Butterfly orchids
(for Maimie)

Maimie, you saw them first –
on a summer afternoon about teatime,
springing up along the path to Tigh na Rois
where elders of the Ross, gathering to share stories
of summers past, walked slowly through a wildflower meadow
between busy road and the burn from the mill leat
that sings as it runs into the arms of the sea, among
bird's-foot trefoil, gowans and meadowsweet –
you called us all to look.

We counted them with delight –
a dozen or more flower spikes flourishing
among the seeding grass, vetches and clover,
white as bird-bones sun-bleached on the strand –
who could remember seeing them last, and when and where?
A harvest of long memories: children of the Ross
laughing among all this greenness and growing,
stepping slowly through the honeyed air,
with every moment counting.

Burns on the cliffs of Burg

(for Cathie)

When I was a bairn, what did I know?
I remember the old folk said
'There are two things that can never be:
the burnie to turn back in its bed,
or buds break on an uprooted tree.'

Now I am old myself and well I know
that broken trees have plenty life in them yet:
and with my own eyes, on days like this, I see
burns on the cliffs of Burg forget
to fall, but fly backwards when big winds blow.

Nevertheless, in my heart of hearts I know
the wisdom in those old words, of burn and tree –
that time can never flow back, nor youth return:
two things that can never be.
Two things that can never be.

Wearing purple
(for Zam)

You're not waiting till you grow old
to wear purple:
you've been wearing it creatively
for so many years;
you're still wearing it right now.

And it's the colour
of blood and wine,
Lent and letting go,
royalty and rejoicing,
love and loss.

Right now, in the season of Easter,
when winter has lasted so long,
it's the colour of fragile birch twigs,
on trees still bare:
purple, a promise of new life.

Throwing an egg over the house
(a family story)

His big hands cradled the egg.
'It shouldn't break,' he said;
we imagined a cartoon splat,
and hoped it would.

Dad took a step back,
measured with his eye,
then – in an arc over the roof –
lobbed the egg high.

Against the blinding blue
the egg flew – and we ran, witnesses
to the landing, unscathed,
as it bounced and rolled on the grass.

Passed it from hand to hand:
its smooth shell full of mystery:
Dad explained that a pocket of air
inside the shell had saved the day.

Ran a control – the egg stayed whole –
until (this was Home Economy)
Mum added less adventurous eggs
and scrambled them for our tea.

How long ago was that? Sixty years.
After thirty we repeated the experiment:
another generation: a different dad,
a new egg. It, too, bounced.

And here and now two children
run and, with subversive wonder,
watch an egg arc against the blue,
and bounce into the future.

In Brighton

(for Linus)

The sea horizon's strung like a washing line
between these white terraces –
taut space beyond the jostle of human lives.

From the front step of your new home
it's the first thing we see: ruled in graphite,
glinting in the sun like sheet metal – ever-present.

You're not a week into the world,
as we take you down steep streets to the sea's edge –
three generations in a procession with a pram,

small boy wrapped in a bright blanket,
with parents passionate to protect you
from chill winds and the world's hard edges.

Suddenly you were delivered into this world;
every day you meet more of it: today, the sea.

Exhilarated, four pairs of lungs breathe in air
that has crossed great distances, while
the waves roll in from that line between sea and sky.

Cocooned, you're rocked in the rhythm of our walking,
eyes open, gazing but not yet focusing –
for you, loving arms, the taste of milk, blurred faces,
heartbeat and voices shape the universe:

for you, right now, the world has no horizons.

Surfing
(for Anna)

Suddenly I see you,
standing up in an impossible place
and being carried away.

Before, I could just make you out,
in a shoal of folk about your age –
waving, laughing, all out of your depth,
playing in the starting-up swell.
I saw how you stretched out your arms like a supplicant,
holding your board, imagined your body tense
as the breaker built up to this moment.

And now, for a drawn breath,
you seem to be on top of it:
even at this distance, I can feel the exhilaration
and the risk
of riding bareback on a galloping wave,
balancing on a knife-edge,
sliding across glass that is shattering,
as the tower you've climbed begins to topple.

This, my child, is your choice, and –
salt stinging my eyes –
I watch you careering between fear and joy,
while I stand still on the safety of the sand.

The voyager
(for Dwin)

I bought this rowing boat from you
because I wanted, simply, to use it –
being a boat-owner was a long way from my mind.
I dreamed of working my way
along these shores you knew so well:
baling and playing in the shallows
then pushing out into deeper water.

For you this boat had no name,
was simply a small and useful vessel.
I freighted her with laughter and tears –
with the name *Hilarity* – but I've not yet
got round to writing that on bows or stern:
right now, what she needs is hands-on care,
scraping, sanding, oiling, coats of paint.

This year too many things have blown my way,
so many contrary currents,
leaving our boat (yours, then mine)
high and dry at the back of the shore,
bleaching in the sun and salt wind.

As you were dying, I was in a far country
among the shepherds, in the mountains.
Now back at sea-level, I stand idly
watching the working boats, running my hand
along this rusty keel, these flaking ribs;

reluctantly, I know it will be next year
before this boat's back in the water.

You'd made a noost in folk's hearts here:
they still keep asking after you,
missing your grin, your words and silences,
your hard-working hands, remembering
with gratitude how you mended, made things grow,
regretting your restlessness: suddenly
you upped anchor, went back to where you began,
then died, too soon. And now I know

that your ashes were launched by loving hands
on the windy moors where once you herded sheep.

You knew more about sheep and boats
and people than I ever will – and it tells.
While I wander the shore, wondering what's to be done
with a nameless boat stranded here, waiting,
for the inspiration or energy of another year,
you're ahead of me – voyaging on,
beyond tides and seasons, beyond words,
through the deep silence of the high fells.

The little waves

(for Erin)

Along the shore, on this March day,
the little breaking waves
take on the pattern of breathing, or heartbeats.

Not the dark rush of blood
which we heard from the womb
as though you were impatient to be born.

Now there's a steadiness
to the pause, fall, withdrawing:
each long sigh and next intake of breath.

Out there, at sea, breakers surge;
with fatal currents, depths we cannot fathom,
or control – we have come through chaos

to where, on what we pray is a safe shore,
arriving ripples fan across the sand,
exploring this new space like little hands.

'The Parlement of foules'

A long poem by Chaucer is based on the idea of a debate among the birds. I never attempted anything so ambitious, but over the last few years on Mull, and on boat trips out to smaller islands like Lunga, I often find myself listening to, watching, wondering at, wanting to learn more about birds – and attempting to write about them. Their calls, their migrations, their beauty in flight, their mysterious lives, speak to me. Signs of the diversity and delight of God's creation, small survivors in a risky world, they humble me and give me hope.

But I'm not an expert; I fail the bird list and the Big Binocular test. This is, after all, an island where folk who flock to see the wildlife know what they are looking for. A couple of years ago we, a group of local poets, were putting together some of our work. Would it sell to visitors? we wondered – and decided that all we needed to do was put on the cover 'May contain eagles'.

Among the birds gathered here, there's a lonely corncrake and an albino blackbird; however, you'll recognise most of the others. It's possible these common birds have something to say to us. But there's not a single eagle.

Seagulls on the strand

A party conference of gulls –
arguments, loud laughter,
fish suppers.

The ringed plover

In a scrape among the stones –
sea pebbles and quarry waste,
scratchy with dried seaweed –
the ringed plover lays her eggs
humble and speckled, hard to see:
right where the sheep wander, where
boots trample, where the boat's keel
was hauled over stones
to the water's edge.

And yet they are still intact.

Meanwhile, like a wind-up toy,
she scuttles about the shore,
dabbling in this and that –
in the small busyness of her life –
as though she'd left no hidden treasure,
no small miracle of survival,
in a scrape among the stones.

Whooper swans

Two white swans
in Bunessan this morning,
riding at anchor between the burn's mouth
and the mudflats –
exotic among ducks and oystercatchers.
They're visitors brought in by the east wind
from Russia, Norway, Iceland: from somewhere
right off our map.

Starting a different story
with their companionable presence;
displaced but full of dignity,
reflecting the snows on Ben More;
and, on the village bay,
writing their question mark.

Listening to Lunga

Who woke the kittiwakes on the sea stack?
White wings,
cries full of surprise.

Rafts of razorbills and guillemots,
shags, geese, common gulls:
commotion!

A groan from the burrow –
teenage puffins
taking a telling off?

Corncrakes creep in bracken
but their rasping calls
bounce back from basalt crags.

Beyond the ruins on Lunga
I heard a lament –
the grey seals singing.

A breathing hush, glassy calm
broken by a boat's throttle
and churning wake.

Peevish oystercatchers
scold heedless incomers:
Eggs! Eggs underfoot!

Hauled in, the anchor chain snores;
on board
we're waking from an island dream.

Engine stops stammering,
sails unfurl, waves kiss our hull …
moving silence.

Iona rookery

This is it, then, as far west
as any rook can feel at home:
what a place to build a nest –
in these trees that keep their heads down
when the wind comes over the crag;
in branches that rock and buck like boats on the bay;
in this skerry of lichened sycamores
amid the swells of machair and moor.

West is best, and this is the furthest west.
And for this building of rooks
(this parliament, colony, community),
this is the way it needs to be:
all the elements are in place –
hoarse voices, twigs to gather, the same old trees;
black wings testing the changing weather,
bright eyes divvying out the space;

and the constant controversy
that keeps them all together.

The flyting

They're a power in the land, these rooks:
a rambunctious presence creating
facts on the ground, taking over ploughed fields,
grubbing about, claiming air space,
contesting nest sites, grabbing attention –
all the time, their argy-bargy.

West is best and we are the furthest west –
the Iona rooks shout, from their community
built on holy ground, or rather in the boughs
of sycamores round the old manse;
riding the gusts, they brag loudly
about their uniqueness, their claim to fame.

But now the truth's out: the rooks of Glendale
over on Skye have the edge – though it's less
than half a degree of longitude.
The north wind carries their mockery to Iona:
Our rookery rocks, our nests are further west,
yes, furthest west, and far and away the best!

The white blackbird

In the billiard room, long windows
overlook gravel and grass and then the sea,
which is not always tame.

Here stuffed birds are imitating life,
shut up in glass cases, after being shot,
their eggs stolen and blown.

In one dark corner, two owls stare
reproachfully from a tree's hollow,
their plumage mottled like the bark.

A diorama of rocks and waves,
surrounds an albino cormorant
looking surprised at itself.

And in a bell-jar, perched on top
of the owl's case, a smaller bird –
familiar, but somehow wrong.

A family story: one day in 1895
a white blackbird appeared, here
in the grounds of the big house.

Imagine it, exploring new-found land:
the raked gravel, rolled lawns,
the boundless sea beyond;

imagine, from a bird so small,
full-throated song,
filling the salt air on that spring day.

Did it make them want to burst out singing:
the family and their guests in the big house,
gazing out through long windows?
The housemaids gathered at the kitchen door,
and the lad who paused as he raked the gravel?
Did they listen with joy, find time to look their fill
at the wonder of a white blackbird?

It was a rare specimen:
so the man of the house shot it.

Sent it off to Inverness,
to be stuffed with skill, labelled with care;
brought it back to spend all the years since
in an empty room – a trophy under glass –
looking like nothing more or less
than a blackbird that has faded with time

with its song silenced.

Swallows at Crianlarich

The sleeper shuffles into Crianlarich
on a grey morning, eyes not quite open yet.
Stepping onto the platform, I feel air from the hills
splash like fresh water in my face

and am startled by a world full of wings:
swallows swooping round the station,
small bodies that jink and dart,
over the down platform, past tearoom signs
and tubs of late-summer flowers,
across lines stretching south to Glasgow,
rails running north across Rannoch Moor –
dancing as though delighted,
maybe with the morning midge-rise,
or simply with all that air

sending out urgent messages on twitter,
low-flying, then looping over and up
to gather on wires with fast-beating hearts:
a new brood testing their wings
in training for the long haul
where lines converge on the horizon,
connecting with another hemisphere

and this in-between place where I've alighted,
paused for breath, is where the tired year
breathes out and blows them far away –
where the young swallows' journey starts.

The Staffa corncrake

I hear there was a single corncrake
on Staffa this year:
'It was calling all summer.'

One calling corncrake could mean a pair –
a mate maybe, who'd also covered
all those air-miles from Africa,
over desert and forest and vast oceans,
seeking out this small island:
a homing hen-bird at his beck and call,
tiptoeing through wildflowers and grasses
to build her nest, and raise her hidden brood.

Or maybe she came over
on a day-trip from Iona,
heard the lonely corncrake calling her name,
crex crex,
louder than the sea music in Fingal's cave,
and stayed.

Maybe there was more than one.

Then why was he calling all summer? *Crex crex* –
while the weather blew in from the Atlantic – *crex crex* –
while the puffins came ashore, and reared their young,
and hungry gulls patrolled the basalt cliffs – *crex crex* –
while cloud-shadows moved across the mountains of Mull

and gannets dived into the scintillating sea – *crex crex* –
calling, calling, *crex crex*,
calling all summer, with no response.

So a day came when he wrote off the summer,
took off and set off alone to his African home –
crex crex, crex crex –
a single corncrake on Staffa this year.

The Penmon robin

Five friends walked a path at Penmon,
in the week before Advent,
and a robin came to see what we were at:

cocked head, feathers fluffed out – surprising
with a blush of red – took wing, landed on
a winter twig, quizzical, sizing us up,

then flew down to our feet; a watchful, trusting
presence, always a few paces ahead,
all the way to St Seiriol's holy well.

We'd come weary and empty-handed –
we had no bread to share – but found
we walked on holy ground on that grey day

and were well-blessed: our pilgrimage
having such steadfast accompaniment:
encouragement every step of the way.

Midwinter wren

Small spark of life,
sheltered by a dry-stone wall
from the life-or-death
winds of winter,
calling 'I'm here, I'm here.'

Little cave-dweller,
from your snug nest
of woven grasses
and borrowed feathers,
bob out now, to tell the world
'I'm here, I'm here!'

High-flier, winter king,
making yourself at home
in unlikely places, finding
the common ground with us;
bright as a three-penny bit
new-minted, you chirp
'I'm here, I'm here!'

Down-to-earth star-child,
such a small presence
to make all the difference:
frail as a single snowflake,
brave as a candle-flame,
singing out
'I'm here, I'm here!'

Listening for larks

You can't help hearing the wild geese –
their wing beats overhead and their strident calls.
You can't help being aware of them, day and night,
wherever they set webfoot, contending over territory,
food, relationships, leadership,
arguing about who's right:
the geese just let you know they're there.

Then listen for the larks –
their shimmering song's subtle,
sometimes lost in the blustering wind
or overlooked by busy minds –
but wonder at how these humble birds persist,
are constant in their life-work of praise.

When you are set foot on unfamiliar tracks,
or trudge along well-trodden ways;
whether in dancing sunshine, or on grey still days;
their song, a canon of joy, fills the air:
listen, the larks are still there.

Writing desk on the shore

At home on the Ross of Mull, I can abandon mundane tasks and walk on a nearby shore, watching and listening to the waves, an experience which puts other concerns into perspective. There's something grounding, reassuring, here. Such places are also full of surprises, though – on Mull I came across a whole lot of household furniture at the back of a beach; in Eastern Australia I thought I was wading in molten gold; on California's west coast, I wondered at the warning 'Don't turn your back on the waves'!

Lighthouses keep our shores safe and the work of the Stevenson family, making its mark on sea and land, is celebrated in other sections of this book. Here I'm playing with technical terms for the subtly different designs of these towers – names which have their own poetry. There's a whole poem, too, in the name of one of our local beaches, a former salmon-fishing station. 'Uisken' is a variant of Gaelic Uisge – an onomatopoeic word meaning water. Walking beside the water at Uisken inspires with all kinds of images, from the sublime to the ridiculous. A few of these are found here. This section ends with the rhythmic breathing of the waves, which underlines much of what I write.

The writing desk

This little brass key
can no longer lock or unlock anything –
but I've put it on my key ring
to remember something lost.

Warmed by my hand,
it's made of solid brass, burnished with verdigris,
carefully turned, worthless now,
all that's left of a home, a way of life:
it's a displaced key.

I found it in a writing desk
that stood for a few hours looking out to sea,
a strange presence on a Hebridean shore:
all the intricate life of the mind
turfed out of doors.

Table and chairs, wardrobe and bed
from Peggy's croft –
with other unwanted things –
in the marram grass on a grey day,
gathered, riddling guests at a beach bonfire,
chattels that had grown old
with woodworm quietly eating them away:
more than one story waiting to be told.

This desk – from long before laptops –
was never a treasured antique, yet, what wealth:
pigeonholes for letters,

a keyhole to keep secrets,
and a long-dry inkwell,
catching the sound of the waves.

Then everything went onto the fire
and before dark the desk was no more.

But for an hour, a gift of time,
seeing the desk standing open on the shore,
I came closer, pulled up a kitchen chair
(also condemned), sat down
and wrote,
being moved to find, then and there,
words for an ending – or more than one –

and here is the key.

Beach pebble

It's going to take time
to smooth down those rough edges –
millennia –
more than a few hard knocks
and total immersion
in the ocean that changes everything:
transformation's possible
but it's going to take time.

Lighthouse design

Conchoid …
across the machair, and the meadows,
the long muted roar of waves breaking
as in the convolutions of a shell.

Hyperbola …
taken to extremes: the sand's bone-white,
strand's length, blue deeps of sky,
sun's strength, flat earth, heaven's height.

Parabola …
does this describe a surfing kite
that's caught the wind or a lapwing's flight?
Symmetry of painting or pot, a poem's ellipse?

Logarithmic …
connections – or dancing in the dark?
So many questions; on the horizon,
is it an answer – or an exclamation mark?

Collaroy beach

It's Pacific, now,
playing with ocean colours –
aquamarine and ultramarine
and, out there, pure peppermint surf.
Further along the beach,
children are running in and out of the shallows
between the lifeguards' flags planted in the sand,
which is improbably golden.

I paddle where the wealth of surf
is spent along the shoreline
(stranding a silver fish, which I toss back)
and, looking down,
see that the water itself is gold,
with coarse grains suspended and swirling,
thixotropic, rich,
heavy with the long story of the sand.

It seems the sun has dissolved in this ocean.
I wade into it, as though panning for ore,
prospecting:
discovering a new world –
a different element –
knee-deep in flowing gold.

Uisken

Uisken – the sound of little waves
skipping along the sea's edge;

Uisken – footprints on wet sand;

Uisken – bustle of working boats
being launched across the shore;

Uisken – hush of wind in the sedge;

Uisken – a long sigh, a goodbye,
as folk left for another land,
or were carried across the moor,
to the cairn of last-look-back;

Uisken – tears on a day of soft rain;

Uisken – a deep in-breath of air;

Uisken – a dram of salt and kelp,
for someone come home again.

Flotsam

So many things come ashore on Uisken beach:
it's where creatures are cast up to rot quietly
among wrack uprooted by storms, roots writhing
like sea-snakes, odd shoes, mermaid's purses
and fishermen's gloves like yellow starfish.

Here's a wrecked gannet,
a goat that must have fallen from the cliffs,
crab claws and carapaces, hollow urchins,
skeletons of fish, rags of flesh,
seals and seal pups, sadly battered,
collateral damage of the gales.

And this, what is it? A flower on the sand –
exotic bloom on a winter's day
where nothing else will grow –
touch it, and discover it's immortal,
where everything else is breaking down
and going back to the elements.

How did this plastic flower get here?
What currents carried it, and from where,
a café table, or a bride's crown?
Or is it the relic of a wreath
tossed overboard to mark a sea burial:
a last message of love?

So many things come ashore at Uisken beach:
dead things and, strangely, signs of life.

A can of worms

In an abandoned bait bucket,
goose-barnacles have set up home
among traces of the original owners –
wavering wraiths of maggots.

This bucket rolling on the tideline
is boiling with busyness, with creatures
to raise goosebumps or make you gag –
what are they like, goose-barnacles?

Pale bivalve shells, like birds' heads
attached to stretching necks of livid flesh
(necks that are really feet) that wag
and grope blindly and squirm,

while the shell-heads turn as though curious,
or gossiping, gape like beaks; greedy,
they compete for the last few maggots:
a tight little colony feeding off each other:

a gaggle of goose-barnacles,
a shellfish village, a can of worms.

WARNING – 'Don't turn your back on the waves'

Don't turn your back on the waves:
however benign this ocean,
seeming to dream under a blue sky
with a long blur of fog way to the west –
let it lull you into a state of security,
call it pacific – but don't
turn your back on the waves.

Those long slow surges
arriving along this coast
find there's a fault line between water and land,
a deep trench in the slithering sand,
a stumbling block, it throws them:
they explode in impotent rage. Don't
turn your back on the waves.

As driftwood is slowly bleached to bone by the sun,
the sand's ground fine
by this fury: time after time
the breakers falling and going to pieces;
and in between freak waves –
sneakers, sleepers –
sweeping in with unexpected force.
Don't turn your back on the waves.

But turn your face to them:
feeling how the ground shakes

with their majestic tread; hear
how seals playing on their steep green slopes
and flocks of gulls call to each other;
see spindrift flying like white feathers
while a fragile rainbow hovers in the air –
don't turn your back on the waves.

Walk by its side

The sea breathes more slowly than you or I –
three human breaths for every shore-long sigh –
we watch it busy with the task in hand,
bringing in kelp to strew along the sand;
rubbing out bird-prints and footprints,
messiness and messages,
our moments of fame, our names:
the sea teaches us that nothing stays the same.
With every wave, with each tide,
It's rearranging, it's changing,
beach-cleaning and finding new meaning.

So come with me, accompany the sea,
learn from it, walk by its side.

Wild Goose Publications, the publishing house of the Iona Community established in the Celtic Christian tradition of Saint Columba, produces books, e-books, CDs and digital downloads on:

- holistic spirituality
- social justice
- political and peace issues
- healing
- innovative approaches to worship
- song in worship, including the work of the Wild Goose Resource Group
- material for meditation and reflection

For more information:

Wild Goose Publications
The Iona Community
21 Carlton Court, Glasgow, G5 9JP, UK

Tel. +44 (0)141 429 7281
e-mail: admin@ionabooks.com

or visit our website at
www.ionabooks.com
for details of all our products and online sales